Break the NORMS and set her FREE

Maryum Khalil

First Published in September 2021

ISBN: 978-93-5427-703-0

BLUEROSE PUBLISHERS

www.bluerosepublishers.com

info@bluerosepublishers.com

+91 8882 898 898

Cover Design:

Shreya Kapoor

Typographic Design:

Ilma Mirza

Distributed by: BlueRose, Amazon, Flipkart

To those who want to cage the women

&

To the women who have already been caged.

Introduction

Having to be a part of a world where
women are still looked down upon
are still bounded in stereotypes,
are still body shamed,
and looked at with disgusting sights
has made me write
what you are and will be reading ahead.
These thoughts are the result of my observation
and I, by no means believe or intend to say
that every society or man is cruel
but some do think of women as
inferior beings or some useable tools
having no worth, no rights of their own, and no dignity
I myself being a girl, find this very disturbing
and so, have decided to talk about some issues
faced by the women due to the irrational thinking of a society
in this very book of poetry.

~Contents~

Part – 3

Her body

Part – 4

Her heart

Part – 5

Her death

Part – 6

For her

And finally, her message to the world

Her message after you succeeded in ruining her belief in herself,

I know I may not be pretty enough

I know I may not be capable enough

I know I may be worthless

I even know that I may be useless

I know that no one actually cares about me when I absent

cause no one seems to care about me when I am present

but I think that you don't know about my heart

that is still beating.

It does feel hurt because of the words you all are speaking.

So, stop discussing my imperfections

cause I know I am not perfect

stop laughing at me because I look like a clown is something

that I have already accepted

by using funny names is how you to me do call

but you don't realize that in the end its just me on my bed alone

with tears in my eyes and a depressed soul

for it isn't you

the one who then experiences those sleepless nights,

those nights that seem dark and abnormally long.

So please stop cause for right now

I know I am a little weak

I know I am not that strong

I feel like a baby new-born

who tends to sleep peaceful nights

and

isn't capable of participating in

this world's ongoing fights.

Swim through…

But dear,

you are only meant to swim through the ocean

you seem to be drowning in.

Part - 1

~ her dreams ~

Fearing flowers.

And just like a flower

she was beautifully delicate

but under a lot of pressure that

she began to suffocate.

For all she ever wanted was to bloom

but her petals were just too scared.

For they knew, if they would spread their colors

under the light of that sky, what would be their fate?

This world would just cut them down ruthlessly

and tear them separate.

Trapped birds

And she could do wonders
but it's you who has been putting an end
to her thoughts and dreams for ages
and now say that a woman can do nothing
but run household and nurse some babies.
But the truth is that since the beginning
you actually feared giving her the freedom to flap
her wings;
you were actually scared.
For you knew she has got enough power
to show the world what a woman can do
once set free from those cages
into the sky, into the air.

Her burdened soul

A heart filled with pain
A mind full of fears
with a burdened soul
and eyes filled with tears
that is how I felt she was
sitting at the bank of that river.
All alone in dark and cold
Looking at the moon she said
"Why am I born,
if I was to be alone forever?"
Then as she lowered her gaze and blinked
one of her tears fell into the river.
She then watched the water flow
and said, "perhaps these are the tears
of the people who have ever cried before."

Buried seeds

And she dreamt of growing into a tree
but instead of sowing that seed of her dreams
you buried it.
Poor her, what an ambitious girl she was
but it took you no time to do away with
her dreams and damage her spirit.
May God protect and shelter everyone
from such an evil culprit.

Seized land

The stars fascinated her

yet she wasn't allowed to admire their beauty.

She had wings but the sky wasn't hers to fly in.

Only because of the beasts

who into the land of her dreams used to break in.

Slaughtered dreams

She dreamt of a life she desired to live

but her hands were tied and mouth silenced

Only because she was a girl who wished

to become like the woman in her dreams

but such a devastating murder it was

of the visions in those eyes

for she was a mind full of creative thoughts

but with the body that was deliberately paralyzed

Set her free, let her fly

If she dreams about flying across the sky

then dear, help her in learning the art of flight.

Instead of cutting down her wings and making her cry.

For she is a bird with a vision of conquering the sky

so set her free and let her fly.

Sunflowers and sunlight

The more you try and trap her,

the hungrier she will get for fulfilling her desires.

For she is like the sunflower craving for the light of that sun

so, let her out at once

before she burns those cages down like how to the wood does fire.

Be the tire of the car to her dreams

And if she has got a mind full of ambitions
with a potential to achieve them
and a strong vision
then be a person who would
help her drive to her destination
and not the one who would
cut her wings and trap her in a prison.

A resolute angel

All that her soul yearns for is simplicity.
A dark night filled with bright stars
away from the noise of that city.
Her torn wings seem to be tired
but are still held together so gracefully.
For she is an angel, who even if broken
just wouldn't give up easily.

Equality

Every person **irrespective of their gender**

should be given enough space

for exercising their own thoughts

and checking their validity.

For this is essential for

the birth of new laws and

enhancing creativity

Her dedication

And whatever she does

Oh! she does it with such sincerity.

Whether it is about running a nation

or bringing up the next one.

No wonder how a delicate young girl

transforms into such a strong & responsible woman.

Part - 2

~ Her self ~

A painted smile

And that smile that she paints every day
on her dull but still beautiful face.
A face carrying those pretty
but swollen eyes weight.
Wrinkled at the forehead due the thoughts
that perhaps keep disturbing her all day.
But that painted smile of hers
still attracts everyone towards her
even those who to her do hate.
But only if this world knew that
it is under this piece of courage that there lays
her actual smile that has since years been dead.

Cuffed with stereotypes

Being a girl is not an easy task
especially because as soon as she is born
she gets bounded in the cuffs of stereotypes.
The weak, the caretaker of the kids,
the cook in the kitchen, etc. etc.
is how she is described.
Oh, these bizarre stereotypes,
They are way over-hyped.

Silenced cry.

She bleeds herself every month

but never expresses her pain

or maybe is not allowed to

saying that

"what will the people say? So have some shame."

So, she silences her cry and

covers it with a bunch of lies wiping her tears away.

Just because of an absurd question that

"What will the people say?"

It's a girl

And just when the doctor said it's a girl,

a wrinkle of disappointment appeared on your forehead.

then leave her is what your mother said.

So, you walked in on her

while she was still laying on that bed

You are of no good & I don't want you

nor the child in your body is what you then said.

In great confusion she asked;

Why do you say so, honey? what happened?

It's a girl, now how will I show my face to this world?

You sounded so 'upset'

How absurd of you?

But still she begged you not to leave yet you left.

After all that she had done for you

you cared nothing, neither about her

nor about the little angle with which you were going to be blessed.

Never in this world, there would exist a person so unfortunate.

However, I wish that when you end up realizing about what you have done,

May you be left with nothing but a burden of never-ending regret.

The birth of a girl is not a disgrace

And then why did you marry a woman?

if having one makes you feel so unlucky

Just because you fear that

you would have to spend all your money

educating her and building her dowry

and ultimately, she would take all of it

into someone else's family.

Such a bizarre thought, I pity.

But can you answer why did you yourself then

demand for an educated woman and tons of dowry

and now that you are being blessed

with a daughter, you seem so worried.

You see this is life honey

you get to harvest the seed you have sown yourself eventually

but remember that

the birth of a girl is not a disgrace for the family

Woman – A precise leader

And with all sincerity
she weaves a warm nest for her family
with elements such as love
and ingredients such as honesty.
She turns a house into a sweet home
and then holds on to it quite firmly.
Whether it is in the moments that bring joy
or during any calamity
She shelters everyone and protects the family.
So be grateful to her,
for before being a wife or a mother
she is a woman of dignity
who knows how to manage her love and loved ones
with great responsibility.

To parents having daughters

And it's a request

don't bring up your daughter in a way

that she regrets to be one.

For constant prioritizing and praising of your boy

while giving her no attention

will just damage her self-esteem and

cause her to mature into an insecure woman.

Not in age but in fate

And no one got the right to look down upon a girl

if she isn't married at the age of twenty- two or forty-eight.

For who are you to decide what is the right age

for her to get married or when does it get late?

Remember all this depends

on the planning of the God;

on what he has written for her in her fate.

Sad marriages

And without caring about her heart

you decide on getting her married

to a man from whom

she doesn't seem to be pleased.

She cries and begs you to stop.

She tells you that she isn't happy

but you shut her up saying that

"what will the people say, for you are a girl

And so, have no right to speak!"

Only if I could understand about

how selfish can these parents ever be?

For all they care about is what will the people think

rather than caring about their own girl's peace

They don't even bother to think

what if she already has someone in her heart

or what if that man would end up being a beast?

Whose fault will it then be?

So please try and get to know

what's in your daughters' heart?

Before you get her married

For she is the one who ultimately has to live with that man

and not the people whose approval you seek.

The death of the innocent

and she was beaten to death

and they said while defending the man

that it must be her fault

but can they answer

what sin did she commit to deserve that?

What law allows such an assault?

Divorced is better than dead

As soon as a woman gets **divorced**
she doesn't transform into a species so new.
This thing is in itself a lot to go through.
So, if you can't comfort her
then you even got no right to treat her as if
she has according to you
turned worthless or has become of no use.
Stop asking her
"Who will marry you now?
How will you live alone?
Was it your fault?
Why couldn't you bear the abuse?
For you are a girl and should have sacrificed
that is how marriages work but what have you done
do you even have a clue?"
It seems as if you would be happier if
she would have stayed in that torture
and ultimately be dead because of that abuse.

Since you aren't ready to accept a divorced
and are giving her a lecture of
how she should have sacrificed herself to death.
How absurd of you?

Colors of a widow.

Who says that colors are forbidden,

for a girl whose husband has died?

For even if he is gone, her heart is still alive

and during the initial stage of this tragedy

she would herself not be interested in getting out of bed

or wearing that glitter of her eyes

But if after years of being in pain

when she decides to start all over again

what is wrong in her wearing colors

whether red or white?

For she is still a human so please don't torture her with your words

or look at her with those disturbing sights

when she wears the colors other than the black and the white.

Don't govern her using their mindset

To all the parents having beautiful daughters

stop fearing about what will the people say

If your daughter isn't married yet

or if she is divorced;

If she wants to marry someone, she loves

or wear red after being widowed;

It's her life so please stop, imposing restrictions on her

just because of the people having a mindset

that is so immoral and so shallow

The song of her choice

And dear,

A woman is not a puppet

who would keep dancing at the order of your fingertips.

For she has also got a heart to choose the song from

and the freedom to create her own steps

Part ~ 3

~her body~

The chapter – her body

And they studied and discussed her

as though she was one of their chapters.

Scribbled upon her with colorful pens and permanent markers

highlighted everything that according to them

was the most important topic out of the whole matter

and by that, I don't refer to her eyes or her smile

for they were those who focused less on the face

and were interested in everything that was below it,

everything that laid down the aisle.

Defaulted visions

What is it in the color of her body
or in the thickness of her skin
In the stretch marks around her waist
or in the acne on her chin?
That forbid you from accepting her the way she is.
For if you abandon her for such things
then my dear, you have made an incorrect choice
cause there is nothing wrong with her
nor has there ever been
but there sure is something wrong
with your vision from the beginning.
For she was, is, and will always,
irrespective of your judgement
remain beautiful from outside and within.

Flowers and flies

And then she was told
it was all your fault,
it was all your mistake,
That someone made their way through you
without your consent and then flew away
For if the colorful flowers scent so good
How can the flies not get attracted to
such an art is what they then say
But dear just remind them that the flies
even sit over the dead flowers that smell no good in any way
So how is it the fault of the flowers or only their mistake
For why doesn't anyone take the responsibility
of keeping the flies in a cage?

Concealed truths

And she was told

"We don't care about what you are going through

For that is nothing so different, many go through the same and remain silent

So why can't you?

So, she silenced her cry

and started hiding her feelings within herself

For she knew

no matter what she says

no one would understand her pain

and so, started pretending that she is okay

and not like before but she has now become a person so new.

but her still fresh wounds were eating her from within herself

but only if anyone knew the truth.

Her storm, her peace

If she can get her calm back

by screaming out the chaos in her

then let her scream.

For storms do lead to a silence

that brings about an internal peace.

Woman body

She is a woman
who has got dreams to work hard for
and visions like nobody
but still she is restricted from going out
just because of her body.
She is looked at with weird sights of greed
as if she is a source of fulfilling needs
Just because of her body.
She is made to feel insecure
even by those who claim to love her a lot
just because of her body.
And what not?
people just seem to be engrossed in a woman body
and so, for those, I just want to say that
She is also human just like you and everybody
and no one is stopping you from admiring
that creation of God as long as you do it respectfully
Remember that she has also got a mind and some visions to conquer,

she also has dreams of making a history

so, stop restricting her,

For a woman is so much more than just a body.

A broken master piece

And she was a masterpiece
ruthlessly broken
yet
gracefully assembled.

Her freedom is her right

Let the woman feel free
to walk on the streets of at least her own locality;
Whether in the light of that sun
or in the darkness of the night at three.
Stop trying to change women and accuse them
for the unfortunate that happens to them
for they aren't the ones who are guilty.
What's actually wrong is mindset of the people
and the absurd norms of the society.

Wrong lessons

Don't teach your children

that women cannot compete with men, cause

if this lesson in their brain gets fit

It would be the reason behind your girl's silence if a victim

and the reason making your boy a fearless culprit.

There is a beauty in your unique

And dear

just because they say your body is different

don't lose your confidence

For remember that there is a beauty in every unique

There is a charm, there is a magnificence.

Part - 4

~ her heart ~

Owner of the most fragile heart

And she holds within her chest
one of the most expensive gem
The heart of hers that has been
broken into pieces by them
Those who fired it with their words
and those who tore it apart
For they don't realize that
'A girl is the owner of the most fragile heart'

Sucked to death

And just like a fly
he got attracted to that flower
made it believe that it was the most beautiful,
the most pretty among all the others.
Then trapped it in his love
that was seemingly meant to last forever
After that broke one of its petals
and said that it was a mistake
that wouldn't happen again, never.
But part by part he kept tearing them apart
And then sucked all of its nectar and vanished forever
Only if someone could have saved that flower

Her love v/s yours

She thought that your love

would be the medicine to her pain

and hers would be to yours.

So, with her love, she started stitching

all those wounds of yours that were badly torn

While you got busy tearing away

all those of her scars that were already cured

or I may say

she nursed your scars while you tore away her heart;

in-short.

Let her speak

You hurt her but never let her express her pain.
For when she does so, you shut her mouth
like a tied rope shutting a sack of grains.
If not to the ones she loves,
then where else should she go
and unveil the cause of her pain
So, let her speak
even if all she would do is just complain.

Her language of love

And she said you goodbye

Hoping to hear, *I won't leave*, in return

but only if you were that clever

to understand her language of love

only if you knew what she had actually meant

For just as you turned, with a broken voice, she said

"don't go, for this is wasn't my intent"

You turned to her in all anger

and called her crazy then

You broke her heart

but she was a woman pretty descent

who wasn't crazy at mind but was crazy about you.

Her fear of losing you made her lost for words.

She wanted to share her world with you

but you didn't even bother to understand her

Her strength

You kept abusing her

yet she kept loving you.

The man who had promised to

protect her and keep her safe

Poor her, she kept giving chances to you

regardless of what you made her go through.

She still loved you

with all the

drops of the blood she had lost because of you

With all the

scars you gifted her and all the bruises so blue.

Oh, her love, it was so pure, it was so true

but Mr. don't mistake her tears for her weakness

cause you would have left a long time ago

if you would be in her shoes

but she didn't

cause **she is a woman and so is stronger than you.**

The Love games

To all the players out there
a girl's heart is not a dice to be rolled
while you play that so-called game of yours,
named love

Don't ruin her faith in love

If you love her with no intention of marrying her

and making her the mother of your kids

then why love her anyways?

do her a favor, instead of ruining her faith in love

have some mercy on her and walk away.

Save your love

And darling if loving him
makes you fall out of love with yourself
then let me tell you that
what you are doing is just spending all your love
at a place that is absolutely worthless.

Be a man

And if she doesn't love you back
don't seek revenge on her please.
Instead, be a man who would
respect her decision and set her free

Give her the reason to love you

If you truly love her
then don't force her to love you
Instead, give her that reason
so, she could make all your dreams come true.
Build the trust in her that you wouldn't leave her
no matter what she might go through.
Assure her that you will always be hers
and then stick to your words
and see how she will then surrender herself to you

Her heart is not a toy

And her heart is not a game to be played with

For if you can't love, can't respect, and can't care

then you have the doors always open for you to walk away

but if you still choose to stay

let me tell you that her heart is a little home

that belongs to the fairies and angles

So don't you dare

turn into a devil

with the intention of using it as one of its prey

He isn't yours to keep

And if it is the body of yours
that he loves you for
Then honey, leave him.
For you are a gem that is worthy of so much more
You are meant to shine and
he is just making your spark dim.

Trust or lust

Stop looking at other women with dirty eyes

that makes them adjust

their clothes and then look back to check if you are

still looking at them in the same manner that just made them disgust.

For why do you keep forgetting that you have also gotten one

with whom you promise to be in love?

So, would you tolerate this happening to her,

this what you keep doing with others?

So please stop, please don't break her trust

and lose her just for the sake of

fulling your awful desire of lust

Memories to those wounds

And once you break her trust
Don't expect the same her again
For some wounds do heal
but the scars to them
still hold the memories that evoke pain.

A gem in the wrong hands

And she was the beauty people died for
yet she chose you
But dear in all the years you spent with her
she kept getting hurt but still never gave up
All she wanted from you was the love
about which you had promised her earlier
She kept begging you but you
didn't even bother to look at her
For you thought that since she is mine
Where else can she go?
But little did you know,
she was a gem that this world
was desperately longing for.

Her artistry

And then,
you tried to burn her heart to ashes
you tried to tear it apart.
You wanted no one to fall in love with her again
so, you tried destroying that magnificent piece of art.
But only if you knew
about how beautifully she could
even carry the scars carved on her heart.

Not just her fault

All she wanted from you was attention
your attention
but you failed
in offering water to the seed of her love
in offering it some air
and so, if she then goes out to seek others
help to keep her heart alive
then how is it only her mistake?

She is your wife, not your slave

You don't buy her the comb she needs, nor a piece of cloth, nor any jewelry

and then complain saying, "Why don't you dress up and get pretty for me?"

You don't provide her with anything and, then don't even let her make her own money.

For you fear that what will the people say if your wife would work outside

but doesn't she work all day, doing the chores of the house and still gets regarded as just a *"housewife."*

For you need to understand that just because a girl is married to you

doesn't make you **the dictator** of her mind and body

or her a slave, who is just meant for cleaning your house and doing your laundry

for getting abused by you and then giving birth to your babies.

Don't forget that she is also a human who has the right to earn for herself and fulfill her necessities

especially when a man like you fails at doing his duties.

She kept you first

And she was healing you
while she was herself in a lot of pain.
Perhaps she needed you more
than you needed her that day.
But even then, didn't utter a word
neither did you get bothered
by her silenced lips nor her tearful eyes;
by her broken voice nor her sudden anger.
She wasn't herself anymore yet
she was doing all that she could to get you better
or I may say that she was drowning herself
while saving you from the water.

Treat her with kindness.

Dear fathers,

The way your daughter will look at a man later

depends on the way you treat her mother.

So better be kind to your wife

for she is also someone else's daughter

Woman – the natures grace

And she is someone who can
move mountains when in love
and cry oceans when betrayed.
Walk over thorns to reach the person in her heart
and just like water shape into the heart
of the man she loves irrespective of its state.
She is what nature is all about
She is its grace.

When she is love.

If you adorn her sky with just a star

She will adorn yours with a million

For

Wanting to give more than she gets in love

is in the nature of a woman

Keep her heart

She must have been in great love with you
if she makes you, her strength.
So, dear kindly keep her heart and
don't make her regret her decision.

Part - 5

~her death~

Sinking soul

And she came to you because she felt safe

She came to you to unveil the secret

that she had been made fun of or was raped.

She was drowning in an ocean of despair.

She came to you so that you could save her from dying in there.

She came to you for help yet you blamed it all on her, how unfair?

But now that she is battling her life with death why do you seem to care?

Her birth among the stars

She woke at night

with stars beside

saw them shedding tears

and so, asked them the reason why?

They seemed reluctant at first

but then replied

"The reason behind these tears is

that someone down there has died.

Someone you know really well

but now as a star has disguised"

They then asked her to look down

before she had realized

about who was the one no more

about who was the one who had actually died

asked her to watch a body being taken to its final destination;

a body experience its last ride

And just after she saw that body getting laid to rest

she looked at her self

at the way she was turning that night a bit bright.

For it was just then that she recognized,

it was her the newborn star;

it was her the person who had just died.

The actual mourner

And it was only the sky that cried over her grave

while the others were busy pretending

that the raindrops on their cheeks were actually their tears.

Trying to show as if they really cared,

as if to them she was so dear.

But only if she could see it herself about

who was actually sad; about who was unhappier?

It was just the clouds, for they were

the only witness to her broken self,

the only witness to her untold fears.

Her honesty – her mistake

And just like a petal

She was beautiful and delicate

But her choice of being true killed her.

Only if she had an escape

only if she knew that her being honest would actually become her biggest mistake

And only if she knew

that the people in this world only love those who are fake

The angle among the devils

And now, why do you all seem to miss her?

why do you all seem to care?

She was right in front of you when she was losing it all

after all the sacrifices she did

and after all the efforts she made.

Not because she was weak

but because she was tired.

She kept trying her best

but it never seemed to fulfill your desires.

Only if she would have lived for herself

the life, in which all she did was serving others.

Only if she would have been selfish like you

perhaps then she would have lived a little longer

You burdened her life with a pile of stereotypes;

You said her, "*you have to remain silent,*

even if you are going through domestic violence

for you are a girl.

There is no need for you to study

all you have to do is get married and take care of the family

for this is the norm of the world"

Still, she kept fighting for her dreams

she kept fighting till her last breath

she was an angel **striving** among the devils

but you just burdened her life to death.

Flowers for her death

And only if he got those flowers
for expressing his love
and not for signifying her death
after she died.
Only if he got them on time
perhaps then she would have lived a little longer,
lived a little more of this beautiful life.

The truth

They could have saved her

But it's like they never wanted

Who was she?

And today if I am to talk about her

I would say that she was that rare beam of sun

that was enough to enlighten a whole dark sky

She was a rare bird that had the most graceful way to fly.

Her dreams, her ambitions and those of her magical thoughts,

they seemed to be the wings to her mind.

She wasn't going to stop,

she dreamt of owning the universe and calling it "mine"

But no one let her, they were all jealous of her

for she was one of the only kinds

but now she is owned by the mud where

she is sleeping with the peace of mind

Only if she had little more breaths

And only if the people were a bit kind

Let her live

Let her live-in peace

before she gets laid to rest in peace

Part - 6

~for her~

What is a woman?

The more you break her,

the stronger she will emerge

For she is a ***woman;***

One of the strongest being

in this world so diverse.

Woman – the builder of nations

Before bounding her in any relation,

before plotting her as a target in your plan,

and before subjecting her to any sort of gender discrimination

understand the fact that ***"a sacrifice"*** isn't her definition

cause before being a woman,

she is still a human, who is capable of building a nation.

Broken yet expensive

And honey,

wear your broken pieces like charms

hanging from a piece of jewelry.

Embrace them with grace

and then see how they enhance your beauty.

Delicately wild

And she may be as delicate as a flower
But is also as powerful as the wild winds

Tenacious soul

She may be a bird with broken wings

with a bruised heart and burnt skin

Still, she will flap her wings, she will fly.

Even though she is aware

that she might fall down a couple of times.

For she believes in the strength of her wings even if broken,

she believes that to give up is an unpardonable crime.

Tears – her unique strength

But honey,

Don’t ever mistake

a woman’s tears for her weakness

For they only signify her

strength and thereby her uniqueness

What can a girl do?

She was made fun of saying

"You are a girl; what can you do?"

Let me answer that for you

she can nurture a soul within herself

and then give birth to it

despite the pain, she has to go through.

She can run businesses but still

manage to look after her kids and take them to school

She is the force that can drive and conquer nations

without needing a man like you.

Honor her

Honor a woman

respect her flaws

appreciate her efforts

and help her grow.

It's okay

Being a girl and

not being able to cook is okay

Being a girl and

not being able to handle a lot of responsibilities is okay

Being a girl

who doesn't know how to handle children yet is also okay

cause my dear I know

you are trying your best every day

and so, perfection doesn't matter

as long as you are trying to manage.

Use your voice

Stop suffering in silence

you weren't given a tongue to keep quiet.

Raise your voice, no matter what they say

fight against the abuse, fight for your right.

To any women who has been though a lot

I know you are hurt
I know you have been through a lot
I know how you feel that you have got no one,
that you are all alone
But dear, let me remind you of the sun
it may take a break but will always
come back and shine brightly all on its own.

Flap your wings

And dear just because of the people
Do not entrap the wings of your mind
within the cage called skull
Set them free and flap them hard
Set them free and flap them high
Let them take you not just till
but even beyond the parameters of the sky

She knows...

Her life could be a mess
yet she would be composed on the outside
She could be pouring all those clouds
of her eyes on her pillow
yet would walk out with a bright smile.
For she knows she has got this
she knows how to walk through a battlefield
with tranquility and still, win the fight

Don't wait for the season

And honey who said that
to be happy we need a reason?
For rain occurs when it has to
It doesn't wait for any season

For those who still think of women as inferior beings

And if this right disturbs you to such an extent

that you decide to disregard it

then you may but just before you do that

let me remind you of the law that governs all the results

and so, give you a chance to think again over what you did decide

This law that truth will always stay alive

even if it was wanted to be kept hidden

like how the cloud sometimes to the sun try to hide

But remember the rays of the truth or something that is right

do manage to escape out like those of the sun, they do strive

and in the end, it's always them those who win the fight

So kindly accept the truth that

! The birth of a girl is not a disgrace to the family
! Divorced girl is better than a dead one
! Colors aren't forbidden for a widow
! Women build nations
! Women are not the only ones responsible for cooking in the kitchen and serving the children
! Women are strong enough to handle themselves so set them independent

Stop following & start creating

Instead of making your brain a store room of information

and following the crowd of traditions

Create your own path and broaden your imagination.

Women rights are human rights

Standing up for women

is standing up for humanity

About the author

Maryum Khalil is a young and imaginative poet. who loves spending time pondering about the tiny details of life. She has just finished college and is going to pursue a bachelor's degree. She has an ambitious and mind filled with creative thoughts and ideas. She began writing poetry at a very young age and enjoys expressing her feelings and thoughts through it. She believes in creating her own way rather than following the crowd. Apart from writing, she has a great interest in music and photography.

www.ingramcontent.com/pod-product-compliance
Ingram Content Group UK Ltd.
Pitfield, Milton Keynes, MK11 3LW, UK
UKHW021648190726
13853UKWH00001B/122